My Dogs
Health Record

This book belongs to

NAME

ADDRESS

CITY   STATE   ZIP

E-MAIL

PHONE

CELL

My Dog

NAME

BREED

COLOR

BIRTH DATE

My Dogs Photo

About My Dog

Information

Spayed / Neutered   Yes / No

Allergies

_____

Illnesses

_____

Injuries

_____

MicroChip

_____

Blood Type

_____

Breed Registration #

_____

Identifying Marks

_____

Anxiety Triggers

_____

Attack Triggers

_____

Favorite Games

_____

Favorite Toys

_____

Feeding Information

_____

Behaviour Issues

_____

Vet Phone Number:

_____

Notes

_____

_____

_____

"A dog is the only
thing on earth
that loves you more
than you
love yourself"

Josh Billings

VET VISITS

DATE : _____

VET NAME : _____

E-MAIL: _____

PHONE: _____

REASON FOR VISIT : _____

TESTS DONE: _____

_____

DIAGNOSIS : _____

TREATMENT : _____

_____

MEDICATION : _____

SHOTS /
VACCINATIONS : _____

_____

_____

_____

VET VISITS

DATE :

VET NAME :

E-MAIL:

PHONE:

REASON FOR VISIT :

TESTS DONE:

DIAGNOSIS :

TREATMENT :

MEDICATION :

SHOTS /
VACCINATIONS :

VET VISITS

DATE :

VET NAME :

E-MAIL:

PHONE:

REASON FOR VISIT :

TESTS DONE:

DIAGNOSIS :

TREATMENT :

MEDICATION :

SHOTS /
VACCINATIONS :

VET VISITS

DATE : _____

VET NAME : _____

E-MAIL: _____

PHONE: _____

REASON FOR VISIT : _____
_____

TESTS DONE: _____
_____
_____

DIAGNOSIS : _____
_____

TREATMENT : _____
_____

MEDICATION : _____
_____

SHOTS / VACCINATIONS : _____
_____
_____
_____

VET VISITS

DATE :

VET NAME :

E-MAIL:

PHONE:

REASON FOR VISIT :

TESTS DONE:

DIAGNOSIS :

TREATMENT :

MEDICATION :

SHOTS /
VACCINATIONS :

VET VISITS

DATE :

VET NAME :

E-MAIL:

PHONE:

REASON FOR VISIT :

TESTS DONE:

DIAGNOSIS :

TREATMENT :

MEDICATION :

SHOTS /
VACCINATIONS :

VET VISITS

DATE :

VET NAME :

E-MAIL:

PHONE:

REASON FOR VISIT :

TESTS DONE:

DIAGNOSIS :

TREATMENT :

MEDICATION :

SHOTS /
VACCINATIONS :

VET VISITS

DATE :

VET NAME :

E-MAIL:

PHONE:

REASON FOR VISIT :

TESTS DONE:

DIAGNOSIS :

TREATMENT :

MEDICATION :

SHOTS /
VACCINATIONS :

VET VISITS

DATE : _____

VET NAME : _____

E-MAIL: _____

PHONE: _____

REASON FOR VISIT : _____
_____

TESTS DONE: _____
_____
_____

DIAGNOSIS : _____
_____

TREATMENT : _____
_____
_____

MEDICATION : _____
_____
_____

SHOTS /
VACCINATIONS : _____
_____
_____

VET VISITS

DATE : _____

VET NAME : _____

E-MAIL: _____

PHONE: _____

REASON FOR VISIT : _____

_____

TESTS DONE: _____

_____

_____

DIAGNOSIS : _____

_____

TREATMENT : _____

_____

_____

MEDICATION : _____

_____

_____

SHOTS /
VACCINATIONS : _____

_____

_____

VET VISITS

DATE :

VET NAME :

E-MAIL:

PHONE:

REASON FOR VISIT :

TESTS DONE:

DIAGNOSIS :

TREATMENT :

MEDICATION :

SHOTS /
VACCINATIONS :

VET VISITS

DATE :

VET NAME :

E-MAIL:

PHONE:

REASON FOR VISIT :

TESTS DONE:

DIAGNOSIS :

TREATMENT :

MEDICATION :

SHOTS /
VACCINATIONS :

16

VET VISITS

DATE :

VET NAME :

E-MAIL:

PHONE:

REASON FOR VISIT :

TESTS DONE:

DIAGNOSIS :

TREATMENT :

MEDICATION :

SHOTS /
VACCINATIONS :

VET VISITS

DATE : _____

VET NAME : _____

E-MAIL: _____

PHONE: _____

REASON FOR VISIT : _____

_____

TESTS DONE: _____

_____

_____

DIAGNOSIS : _____

_____

TREATMENT : _____

_____

_____

MEDICATION : _____

_____

_____

SHOTS /
VACCINATIONS : _____

_____

_____

VET VISITS

DATE :

VET NAME :

E-MAIL:

PHONE:

REASON FOR VISIT :

TESTS DONE:

DIAGNOSIS :

TREATMENT :

MEDICATION :

SHOTS /
VACCINATIONS :

VET VISITS

DATE :

VET NAME :

E-MAIL:

PHONE:

REASON FOR VISIT :

TESTS DONE:

DIAGNOSIS :

TREATMENT :

MEDICATION :

SHOTS /
VACCINATIONS :

VET VISITS

DATE :

VET NAME :

E-MAIL:

PHONE:

REASON FOR VISIT :

TESTS DONE:

DIAGNOSIS :

TREATMENT :

MEDICATION :

SHOTS /
VACCINATIONS :

21

VET VISITS

DATE :

VET NAME :

E-MAIL:

PHONE:

REASON FOR VISIT :

TESTS DONE:

DIAGNOSIS :

TREATMENT :

MEDICATION :

SHOTS /
VACCINATIONS :

VET VISITS

DATE :

VET NAME :

E-MAIL:

PHONE:

REASON FOR VISIT :

TESTS DONE:

DIAGNOSIS :

TREATMENT :

MEDICATION :

SHOTS /
VACCINATIONS :

VET VISITS

DATE :

VET NAME :

E-MAIL:

PHONE:

REASON FOR VISIT :

TESTS DONE:

DIAGNOSIS :

TREATMENT :

MEDICATION :

SHOTS /
VACCINATIONS :

24

VET VISITS

DATE :

VET NAME :

E-MAIL:

PHONE:

REASON FOR VISIT :

TESTS DONE:

DIAGNOSIS :

TREATMENT :

MEDICATION :

SHOTS /
VACCINATIONS :

25

VET VISITS

DATE :

VET NAME :

E-MAIL:

PHONE:

REASON FOR VISIT :

TESTS DONE:

DIAGNOSIS :

TREATMENT :

MEDICATION :

SHOTS /
VACCINATIONS :

VET VISITS

DATE :

VET NAME :

E-MAIL:

PHONE:

REASON FOR VISIT :

TESTS DONE:

DIAGNOSIS :

TREATMENT :

MEDICATION :

SHOTS /
VACCINATIONS :

VET VISITS

DATE :

VET NAME :

E-MAIL:

PHONE:

REASON FOR VISIT :

TESTS DONE:

DIAGNOSIS :

TREATMENT :

MEDICATION :

SHOTS /
VACCINATIONS :

28

VET VISITS

DATE :

VET NAME :

E-MAIL:

PHONE:

REASON FOR VISIT :

TESTS DONE:

DIAGNOSIS :

TREATMENT :

MEDICATION :

SHOTS /
VACCINATIONS :

VET VISITS

DATE :

VET NAME :

E-MAIL:

PHONE:

REASON FOR VISIT :

TESTS DONE:

DIAGNOSIS :

TREATMENT :

MEDICATION :

SHOTS /
VACCINATIONS :

VET VISITS

DATE :

VET NAME :

E-MAIL:

PHONE:

REASON FOR VISIT :

TESTS DONE:

DIAGNOSIS :

TREATMENT :

MEDICATION :

SHOTS /
VACCINATIONS :

VET VISITS

DATE :

VET NAME :

E-MAIL:

PHONE:

REASON FOR VISIT :

TESTS DONE:

DIAGNOSIS :

TREATMENT :

MEDICATION :

SHOTS /
VACCINATIONS :

VET VISITS

DATE :

VET NAME :

E-MAIL:

PHONE:

REASON FOR VISIT :

TESTS DONE:

DIAGNOSIS :

TREATMENT :

MEDICATION :

SHOTS /
VACCINATIONS :

VET VISITS

DATE :

VET NAME :

E-MAIL:

PHONE:

REASON FOR VISIT :

TESTS DONE:

DIAGNOSIS :

TREATMENT :

MEDICATION :

SHOTS /
VACCINATIONS :

VET VISITS

DATE :

VET NAME :

E-MAIL:

PHONE:

REASON FOR VISIT :

TESTS DONE:

DIAGNOSIS :

TREATMENT :

MEDICATION :

SHOTS /
VACCINATIONS :

35

VET VISITS

DATE :

VET NAME :

E-MAIL:

PHONE:

REASON FOR VISIT :

TESTS DONE:

DIAGNOSIS :

TREATMENT :

MEDICATION :

SHOTS /
VACCINATIONS :

VET VISITS

DATE :

VET NAME :

E-MAIL:

PHONE:

REASON FOR VISIT :

TESTS DONE:

DIAGNOSIS :

TREATMENT :

MEDICATION :

SHOTS /
VACCINATIONS :

VET VISITS

DATE :

VET NAME :

E-MAIL:

PHONE:

REASON FOR VISIT :

TESTS DONE:

DIAGNOSIS :

TREATMENT :

MEDICATION :

SHOTS /
VACCINATIONS :

VET VISITS

DATE :

VET NAME :

E-MAIL:

PHONE:

REASON FOR VISIT :

TESTS DONE:

DIAGNOSIS :

TREATMENT :

MEDICATION :

SHOTS / VACCINATIONS :

VET VISITS

DATE :

VET NAME :

E-MAIL:

PHONE:

REASON FOR VISIT :

TESTS DONE:

DIAGNOSIS :

TREATMENT :

MEDICATION :

SHOTS /
VACCINATIONS :

VET VISITS

DATE :

VET NAME :

E-MAIL:

PHONE:

REASON FOR VISIT :

TESTS DONE:

DIAGNOSIS :

TREATMENT :

MEDICATION :

SHOTS /
VACCINATIONS :

41

VET VISITS

DATE :

VET NAME :

E-MAIL:

PHONE:

REASON FOR VISIT :

TESTS DONE:

DIAGNOSIS :

TREATMENT :

MEDICATION :

SHOTS /
VACCINATIONS :

42

VET VISITS

DATE :

VET NAME :

E-MAIL:

PHONE:

REASON FOR VISIT :

TESTS DONE:

DIAGNOSIS :

TREATMENT :

MEDICATION :

SHOTS /
VACCINATIONS :

VET VISITS

DATE :

VET NAME :

E-MAIL:

PHONE:

REASON FOR VISIT :

TESTS DONE:

DIAGNOSIS :

TREATMENT :

MEDICATION :

SHOTS /
VACCINATIONS :

VET VISITS

DATE :

VET NAME :

E-MAIL:

PHONE:

REASON FOR VISIT :

TESTS DONE:

DIAGNOSIS :

TREATMENT :

MEDICATION :

SHOTS /
VACCINATIONS :

45

VET VISITS

DATE :

VET NAME :

E-MAIL:

PHONE:

REASON FOR VISIT :

TESTS DONE:

DIAGNOSIS :

TREATMENT :

MEDICATION :

SHOTS /
VACCINATIONS :

VET VISITS

DATE :

VET NAME :

E-MAIL:

PHONE:

REASON FOR VISIT :

TESTS DONE:

DIAGNOSIS :

TREATMENT :

MEDICATION :

SHOTS /
VACCINATIONS :

47

VET VISITS

DATE :

VET NAME :

E-MAIL:

PHONE:

REASON FOR VISIT :

TESTS DONE:

DIAGNOSIS :

TREATMENT :

MEDICATION :

SHOTS /
VACCINATIONS :

VET VISITS

DATE : _____

VET NAME : _____

E-MAIL: _____

PHONE: _____

REASON FOR VISIT : _____

TESTS DONE: _____

DIAGNOSIS : _____

TREATMENT : _____

MEDICATION : _____

SHOTS /
VACCINATIONS : _____

VET VISITS

DATE :

VET NAME :

E-MAIL:

PHONE:

REASON FOR VISIT :

TESTS DONE:

DIAGNOSIS :

TREATMENT :

MEDICATION :

SHOTS /
VACCINATIONS :

VET VISITS

DATE :

VET NAME :

E-MAIL:

PHONE:

REASON FOR VISIT :

TESTS DONE:

DIAGNOSIS :

TREATMENT :

MEDICATION :

SHOTS /
VACCINATIONS :

51

VET VISITS

DATE :

VET NAME :

E-MAIL:

PHONE:

REASON FOR VISIT :

TESTS DONE:

DIAGNOSIS :

TREATMENT :

MEDICATION :

SHOTS /
VACCINATIONS :

VET VISITS

DATE :

VET NAME :

E-MAIL:

PHONE:

REASON FOR VISIT :

TESTS DONE:

DIAGNOSIS :

TREATMENT :

MEDICATION :

SHOTS /
VACCINATIONS :

53

VET VISITS

DATE : _____

VET NAME : _____

E-MAIL: _____

PHONE: _____

REASON FOR VISIT : _____

TESTS DONE: _____

DIAGNOSIS : _____

TREATMENT : _____

MEDICATION : _____

SHOTS /
VACCINATIONS : _____

VET VISITS

DATE : _____

VET NAME : _____

E-MAIL: _____

PHONE: _____

REASON FOR VISIT : _____

_____

TESTS DONE: _____

_____

_____

DIAGNOSIS : _____

_____

TREATMENT : _____

_____

_____

_____

MEDICATION : _____

_____

_____

_____

SHOTS /
VACCINATIONS : _____

_____

_____

_____

VET VISITS

DATE :

VET NAME :

E-MAIL:

PHONE:

REASON FOR VISIT :

TESTS DONE:

DIAGNOSIS :

TREATMENT :

MEDICATION :

SHOTS /
VACCINATIONS :

VET VISITS

DATE :

VET NAME :

E-MAIL:

PHONE:

REASON FOR VISIT :

TESTS DONE:

DIAGNOSIS :

TREATMENT :

MEDICATION :

SHOTS /
VACCINATIONS :

VET VISITS

DATE :

VET NAME :

E-MAIL:

PHONE:

REASON FOR VISIT :

TESTS DONE:

DIAGNOSIS :

TREATMENT :

MEDICATION :

SHOTS /
VACCINATIONS :

VET VISITS

DATE :

VET NAME :

E-MAIL:

PHONE:

REASON FOR VISIT :

TESTS DONE:

DIAGNOSIS :

TREATMENT :

MEDICATION :

SHOTS /
VACCINATIONS :

59

VET VISITS

DATE :

VET NAME :

E-MAIL:

PHONE:

REASON FOR VISIT :

TESTS DONE:

DIAGNOSIS :

TREATMENT :

MEDICATION :

SHOTS /
VACCINATIONS :

VET VISITS

DATE :

VET NAME :

E-MAIL:

PHONE:

REASON FOR VISIT :

TESTS DONE:

DIAGNOSIS :

TREATMENT :

MEDICATION :

SHOTS /
VACCINATIONS :

VET VISITS

DATE : _____

VET NAME : _____

E-MAIL: _____

PHONE: _____

REASON FOR VISIT : _____

TESTS DONE: _____

DIAGNOSIS : _____

TREATMENT : _____

MEDICATION : _____

SHOTS /
VACCINATIONS : _____

VET VISITS

DATE :

VET NAME :

E-MAIL:

PHONE:

REASON FOR VISIT :

TESTS DONE:

DIAGNOSIS :

TREATMENT :

MEDICATION :

SHOTS /
VACCINATIONS :

VET VISITS

DATE :

VET NAME :

E-MAIL:

PHONE:

REASON FOR VISIT :

TESTS DONE:

DIAGNOSIS :

TREATMENT :

MEDICATION :

SHOTS /
VACCINATIONS :

VET VISITS

DATE :

VET NAME :

E-MAIL:

PHONE:

REASON FOR VISIT :

TESTS DONE:

DIAGNOSIS :

TREATMENT :

MEDICATION :

SHOTS /
VACCINATIONS :

VET VISITS

DATE :

VET NAME :

E-MAIL:

PHONE:

REASON FOR VISIT :

TESTS DONE:

DIAGNOSIS :

TREATMENT :

MEDICATION :

SHOTS /
VACCINATIONS :

VET VISITS

DATE :

VET NAME :

E-MAIL:

PHONE:

REASON FOR VISIT :

TESTS DONE:

DIAGNOSIS :

TREATMENT :

MEDICATION :

SHOTS /
VACCINATIONS :

VET VISITS

DATE : _____

VET NAME : _____

E-MAIL: _____

PHONE: _____

REASON FOR VISIT : _____

TESTS DONE: _____

DIAGNOSIS : _____

TREATMENT : _____

MEDICATION : _____

SHOTS /
VACCINATIONS : _____

VET VISITS

DATE :

VET NAME :

E-MAIL:

PHONE:

REASON FOR VISIT :

TESTS DONE:

DIAGNOSIS :

TREATMENT :

MEDICATION :

SHOTS /
VACCINATIONS :

VET VISITS

DATE : _____

VET NAME : _____

E-MAIL: _____

PHONE: _____

REASON FOR VISIT : _____

_____

TESTS DONE: _____

_____

_____

DIAGNOSIS : _____

_____

TREATMENT : _____

_____

_____

MEDICATION : _____

_____

_____

SHOTS /
VACCINATIONS : _____

_____

_____

VET VISITS

DATE :

VET NAME :

E-MAIL:

PHONE:

REASON FOR VISIT :

TESTS DONE:

DIAGNOSIS :

TREATMENT :

MEDICATION :

SHOTS /
VACCINATIONS :

VET VISITS

DATE :

VET NAME :

E-MAIL:

PHONE:

REASON FOR VISIT :

TESTS DONE:

DIAGNOSIS :

TREATMENT :

MEDICATION :

SHOTS /
VACCINATIONS :

VET VISITS

DATE : _____

VET NAME : _____

E-MAIL: _____

PHONE: _____

REASON FOR VISIT : _____

_____

TESTS DONE: _____

_____

_____

DIAGNOSIS : _____

_____

TREATMENT : _____

_____

_____

MEDICATION : _____

_____

_____

SHOTS /
VACCINATIONS : _____

_____

_____

_____

VET VISITS

DATE :

VET NAME :

E-MAIL:

PHONE:

REASON FOR VISIT :

TESTS DONE:

DIAGNOSIS :

TREATMENT :

MEDICATION :

SHOTS /
VACCINATIONS :

VET VISITS

DATE :

VET NAME :

E-MAIL:

PHONE:

REASON FOR VISIT :

TESTS DONE:

DIAGNOSIS :

TREATMENT :

MEDICATION :

SHOTS /
VACCINATIONS :

VET VISITS

DATE :

VET NAME :

E-MAIL:

PHONE:

REASON FOR VISIT :

TESTS DONE:

DIAGNOSIS :

TREATMENT :

MEDICATION :

SHOTS /
VACCINATIONS :

VET VISITS

DATE :

VET NAME :

E-MAIL:

PHONE:

REASON FOR VISIT :

TESTS DONE:

DIAGNOSIS :

TREATMENT :

MEDICATION :

SHOTS /
VACCINATIONS :

VET VISITS

DATE :

VET NAME :

E-MAIL:

PHONE:

REASON FOR VISIT :

TESTS DONE:

DIAGNOSIS :

TREATMENT :

MEDICATION :

SHOTS /
VACCINATIONS :

VET VISITS

DATE : _____

VET NAME : _____

E-MAIL: _____

PHONE: _____

REASON FOR VISIT : _____

_____

TESTS DONE: _____

_____

_____

DIAGNOSIS : _____

_____

TREATMENT : _____

_____

_____

MEDICATION : _____

_____

_____

SHOTS /
VACCINATIONS : _____

_____

_____

VET VISITS

DATE :

VET NAME :

E-MAIL:

PHONE:

REASON FOR VISIT :

TESTS DONE:

DIAGNOSIS :

TREATMENT :

MEDICATION :

SHOTS /
VACCINATIONS :

VET VISITS

DATE :

VET NAME :

E-MAIL:

PHONE:

REASON FOR VISIT :

TESTS DONE:

DIAGNOSIS :

TREATMENT :

MEDICATION :

SHOTS /
VACCINATIONS :

VET VISITS

DATE :

VET NAME :

E-MAIL:

PHONE:

REASON FOR VISIT :

TESTS DONE:

DIAGNOSIS :

TREATMENT :

MEDICATION :

SHOTS /
VACCINATIONS :

VET VISITS

DATE :

VET NAME :

E-MAIL:

PHONE:

REASON FOR VISIT :

TESTS DONE:

DIAGNOSIS :

TREATMENT :

MEDICATION :

SHOTS /
VACCINATIONS :

VET VISITS

DATE :

VET NAME :

E-MAIL:

PHONE:

REASON FOR VISIT :

TESTS DONE:

DIAGNOSIS :

TREATMENT :

MEDICATION :

SHOTS /
VACCINATIONS :

VET VISITS

DATE :

VET NAME :

E-MAIL:

PHONE:

REASON FOR VISIT :

TESTS DONE:

DIAGNOSIS :

TREATMENT :

MEDICATION :

SHOTS /
VACCINATIONS :

85

VET VISITS

DATE :

VET NAME :

E-MAIL:

PHONE:

REASON FOR VISIT :

TESTS DONE:

DIAGNOSIS :

TREATMENT :

MEDICATION :

SHOTS /
VACCINATIONS :

86

VET VISITS

DATE :

VET NAME :

E-MAIL:

PHONE:

REASON FOR VISIT :

TESTS DONE:

DIAGNOSIS :

TREATMENT :

MEDICATION :

SHOTS /
VACCINATIONS :

VET VISITS

DATE :

VET NAME :

E-MAIL:

PHONE:

REASON FOR VISIT :

TESTS DONE:

DIAGNOSIS :

TREATMENT :

MEDICATION :

SHOTS /
VACCINATIONS :

VET VISITS

DATE :

VET NAME :

E-MAIL:

PHONE:

REASON FOR VISIT :

TESTS DONE:

DIAGNOSIS :

TREATMENT :

MEDICATION :

SHOTS /
VACCINATIONS :

VET VISITS

DATE :

VET NAME :

E-MAIL:

PHONE:

REASON FOR VISIT :

TESTS DONE:

DIAGNOSIS :

TREATMENT :

MEDICATION :

SHOTS /
VACCINATIONS :

VET VISITS

DATE : _____

VET NAME : _____

E-MAIL: _____

PHONE: _____

REASON FOR VISIT : _____
_____

TESTS DONE: _____
_____
_____

DIAGNOSIS : _____
_____

TREATMENT : _____
_____
_____

MEDICATION : _____
_____
_____

SHOTS /
VACCINATIONS : _____
_____
_____

91

VET VISITS

DATE :

VET NAME :

E-MAIL:

PHONE:

REASON FOR VISIT :

TESTS DONE:

DIAGNOSIS :

TREATMENT :

MEDICATION :

SHOTS /
VACCINATIONS :

VET VISITS

DATE :

VET NAME :

E-MAIL:

PHONE:

REASON FOR VISIT :

TESTS DONE:

DIAGNOSIS :

TREATMENT :

MEDICATION :

SHOTS /
VACCINATIONS :

VET VISITS

DATE :

VET NAME :

E-MAIL:

PHONE:

REASON FOR VISIT :

TESTS DONE:

DIAGNOSIS :

TREATMENT :

MEDICATION :

SHOTS /
VACCINATIONS :

94

VET VISITS

DATE :

VET NAME :

E-MAIL:

PHONE:

REASON FOR VISIT :

TESTS DONE:

DIAGNOSIS :

TREATMENT :

MEDICATION :

SHOTS /
VACCINATIONS :

VET VISITS

DATE :

VET NAME :

E-MAIL:

PHONE:

REASON FOR VISIT :

TESTS DONE:

DIAGNOSIS :

TREATMENT :

MEDICATION :

SHOTS /
VACCINATIONS :

96

VET VISITS

DATE :

VET NAME :

E-MAIL:

PHONE:

REASON FOR VISIT :

TESTS DONE:

DIAGNOSIS :

TREATMENT :

MEDICATION :

SHOTS /
VACCINATIONS :

VET VISITS

DATE :

VET NAME :

E-MAIL:

PHONE:

REASON FOR VISIT :

TESTS DONE:

DIAGNOSIS :

TREATMENT :

MEDICATION :

SHOTS /
VACCINATIONS :

98

VET VISITS

DATE :

VET NAME :

E-MAIL:

PHONE:

REASON FOR VISIT :

TESTS DONE:

DIAGNOSIS :

TREATMENT :

MEDICATION :

SHOTS /
VACCINATIONS :

VET VISITS

DATE :

VET NAME :

E-MAIL:

PHONE:

REASON FOR VISIT :

TESTS DONE:

DIAGNOSIS :

TREATMENT :

MEDICATION :

SHOTS /
VACCINATIONS :

VET VISITS

DATE :

VET NAME :

E-MAIL:

PHONE:

REASON FOR VISIT :

TESTS DONE:

DIAGNOSIS :

TREATMENT :

MEDICATION :

SHOTS /
VACCINATIONS :

VET VISITS

DATE :

VET NAME :

E-MAIL:

PHONE:

REASON FOR VISIT :

TESTS DONE:

DIAGNOSIS :

TREATMENT :

MEDICATION :

SHOTS /
VACCINATIONS :

VET VISITS

DATE : _____

VET NAME : _____

E-MAIL: _____

PHONE: _____

REASON FOR VISIT : _____

_____

TESTS DONE: _____

_____

_____

DIAGNOSIS : _____

_____

TREATMENT : _____

_____

_____

MEDICATION : _____

_____

_____

SHOTS /
VACCINATIONS : _____

_____

_____

_____

VET VISITS

DATE :

VET NAME :

E-MAIL:

PHONE:

REASON FOR VISIT :

TESTS DONE:

DIAGNOSIS :

TREATMENT :

MEDICATION :

SHOTS /
VACCINATIONS :

VET VISITS

DATE :

VET NAME :

E-MAIL:

PHONE:

REASON FOR VISIT :

TESTS DONE:

DIAGNOSIS :

TREATMENT :

MEDICATION :

SHOTS /
VACCINATIONS :

VET VISITS

DATE :

VET NAME :

E-MAIL:

PHONE:

REASON FOR VISIT :

TESTS DONE:

DIAGNOSIS :

TREATMENT :

MEDICATION :

SHOTS /
VACCINATIONS :

VET VISITS

DATE :

VET NAME :

E-MAIL:

PHONE:

REASON FOR VISIT :

TESTS DONE:

DIAGNOSIS :

TREATMENT :

MEDICATION :

SHOTS /
VACCINATIONS :

Vaccination Schedule for Dogs

Vaccine	First Puppy Vaccination	Initial adult Vaccination	Booster	Comments
Rabies 1-year	Single dose, as early as 3 months of age. Age depends on state regulations.	Single Dose	Annual	Core dog vaccine. Rabies is Fatal to Dogs
Rabies 3-year	Single dose, as early as 3 months of age. Age depends on state regulations	Single dose	A second vaccination after 1 year, then boosters every 3 years	Core dog vaccine.
Distemper	At least 3 doses, between 6 and 16 weeks of age	2 doses, 3-4 weeks apart	Boost 1 year after completing initial series. Boost every 3 years or more often	Core dog vaccine. Distemper virus is a severe disease that may cause permanent brain damage.
Parvovirus	3 doses, given between 6 and 16 weeks of age	2 doses, 3-4 weeks apart	Booster 1 year after completing the initial series, Boost every 3 years or more often	Core dog vaccine. Virus is contagious, and can cause severe vomiting and bloody diarrhea. Parvo is fatal if untreated.
Adnovrus, type 1 (CAV-1, canine hepatitis)	3 doses, between 6 and 16 weeks of age	2 doses, 3-4 weeks apart	Boost 1 year after completing the initial series, Boost every 3 years or more often	Core dog vaccine. Can lead to severe liver damage, and death.
Adenovirus, type 2 (CAV-2, kennel cough)	doses, between 6 and 16 weeks of age	2 doses, 3-4 weeks apart	Boost 1 year after completing the initial series, Boost every 3 years or more often	Core dog vaccine.

Vaccine	First Puppy Vaccination	Initial adult Vaccination	Booster	Comments
Parainfluenza	First does at 6-8 weeks of age, then every 3-4 weeks until 12-14 weeks old	1 dose	Boost after 1 year, Boost every 3 years	Non-core dog vaccine. Not fatal
Bordetella bronchiseptica (kennel cough)	2 doses usually	1 dose of the oral product, or 2 doses of the injected product	Annual or 6-month .	Non-core dog vaccine. Not fatal
Lyme disease	1 dose, administered as early as 9 weeks, with a second dose 2-4 weeks later	2 doses, 2-4 weeks apart	May be needed annually, prior to the start of tick season	Non-core dog vaccine. Only for dogs with a high risk for exposure to Lyme disease-ticks.
Leptospirosis	First dose as early as 8 weeks, with a second dose 2-4 weeks later	2 doses, 2-4 weeks apart	Annually for dogs in high-risk areas	*Non-core dog vaccine.* *Usually in high risk areas*
Adnovrus, type 1 (CAV-1, canine hepatitis)	3 doses, between 6 and 16 weeks of age	2 doses, 3-4 weeks apart	Boost 1 year after completing the initial series, Boost every 3 years or more often	Core dog vaccine. Can lead to severe liver damage, and death.
Canine influenza	First dose as early as 6-8 weeks; second dose 2-4 weeks later	2 doses, 2-4 weeks apart	Yearly	*Non-core dog vaccine.*

Pet Poison Help

In the event that you believe that your pet has been poisoned – get help immediately.

Plants that are poisonous to dogs

https://www.aspca.org/pet-care/animal-poison-control/dogs-plant-list

People foods that are poisonous to dogs

https://www.aspca.org/pet-care/animal-poison-control/people-foods-avoid-feeding-your-pets

The following services are available 24 /7 and do incur a fee for use

ASPCA Animal Poison Control Center (**ASPCA-APCC**)	1.888.426.4435.	24/7 365 days a year Fee $65 fee (2019)
Pet Poison Helpline (**PPH**)	1.800.213.6680	24/7 365 days a year Fee $59 (2019)
Pets & Pesticides	1.800.858.7378	Non emergency only

Notes

Notes